# DAILY PRACTICES

THE
DREAM
LIFE
PROJECT

Copyright © 2024 Cecilia Huang
First published 2024
The Dream Life Project
https://thedreamlifeproject.co
ISBN: 978-1-7638175-2-4

All rights reserved. No parts of the publication may be reproduced, distributed, or transmitted in any form or by any means including photocopying, recording, or other electronic or mechanical methods without prior written permission from the publisher.

Design and layout by Cecilia Huang

101 tiny steps to reclaim compassion

# DAILY PRACTICES

CECILIA HUANG

# introduction

Compassion isn't confined to rare moments of indulgence or occasional escapes; it's a daily practice that weaves together joy and discipline. In this book, I'm thrilled to share with you how tiny, intentional steps can transform your relationship with yourself and guide you towards a life filled with fulfilment and happiness.

True compassion is about more than just treating yourself to a spa day or a night out. It's about consistently valuing, respecting, and nourishing yourself in ways that support the direction you want your life to take. It means prioritising your needs, setting boundaries, and extending to yourself the same kindness that you would offer to someone you deeply care about. This book is an invitation to embrace a compassion mindset where taking care of yourself becomes a natural, enriching part of your daily routine.

Throughout these pages, you'll discover a variety of daily practices designed to make compassion an integral part of your life. From the simplicity of starting your day with an intention to the joy of savouring quiet moments and the stability of nurturing meaningful relationships, these tiny steps are powerful tools for creating a compassionate lifestyle. We'll explore how these practices can help you find balance, meaning, and a deeper connection with yourself, while also making space for joy and fulfilment in your everyday life.

As you embark on this journey, I hope you find inspiration and encouragement in these practices. Each tiny step is a step toward rediscovering your worth, embracing who you are, and celebrating the unique individual you've always been. Here's to nurturing yourself with love and creating a life that truly reflects your dreams and desires.

*Cecilia*

When you are compassionate with yourself, you trust in your soul, which you let guide your life. You soul knows the geography of your destiny better than you do.

JOHN O'DONOHUE

1

# look for meaning

Each experience carries within it a valuable lesson waiting to be uncovered. Self-growth often requires patience, introspection, and a willingness to embrace the teachings, allowing them to shape you into the best version of yourself.

2

# consider your mindset

Obstacles in life can either impede your progress or propel you forward, depending on your perspective. Navigate the obstacles in your path, don't allow them to hinder your journey, and harness their potential to propel you towards your goals.

3

# practice acceptance

There are rough patches in life, pain, fear, and suffering included. However, not all tough times are bad experiences. Sometimes, they're like the fertilizer for your personal growth. Pain teaches you stuff, fear can make you brave, and suffering is like a boot camp for inner strength.

4

# experience everything

Grow your resilience like a rubber band, stretch, bend, but never break. Allow yourself to feel the full spectrum of emotions, even when it hurts, and still finding the strength to bounce back, no matter how many times life knocks you down.

5

# accept your fear

Life is like riding a rollercoaster, sometimes you're feeling brave, ready to conquer anything, and other times, fear creeps in like that unexpected drop. It's totally okay to be brave and afraid at the same time. Face your fears head-on, even when your knees are shaking.

6

# foster the idea of 'good enough'

'Good' is good enough. Don't let perfect be the enemy of good. You're more likely to encounter setbacks if you hold yourself to impossibly high standards. Perfectionism is an attitude to lose. Strive for continuous improvement, each step forward is a success.

7

# control your destiny

Sometimes you may feel like you're strapped in and just hanging on. Remember, you're not defined by the ups and downs. You're the authors of your own story, with the power to rewrite the plot whenever you choose. Learn from the ride, own your story and rewrite the script with courage and resilience.

8

# see yourself clearly

Put yourself out in the open. There's no room for living by comparison with others. You are allowed to not meeting impossible goals or standards. There's just you: your authentic self, who you really are. When you honestly know that person, then you can meet her needs.

9

# don't let guilt run the show

You feel guilty because you perceive that self-care is indulgent. In fact, self-care equals self-respect. Respect yourself, then you'll take care of yourself. Drop the guilt. By looking after yourself, you are looking after your family and future too.

10

# stand out

True impact often comes from standing apart, from daring to think and act differently. When you embrace your uniqueness, you step into your potential to make a difference. It's easy to blend in, but it's the bold choice to be authentic that allows you to bring something truly valuable to the world.

*No one ever made a difference by being like everyone else.*

P. T. BARNUM

11

# accept yourself

Accept everything about yourself. No apologies, no regrets. Embrace every part of who you are, your strengths, flaws, triumphs, and mistakes. By fully accepting yourself, you grant permission to live without the weight of others' opinions. Honour your journey and love yourself unconditionally.

12

# define true self-care

True self-care involves making intentional choices that prioritise your physical, mental, and emotional wellbeing. When you create a life that brings you joy, purpose, and fulfilment, you don't need to escape from it.

13

# take care of yourself

Taking care of yourself is a lifelong journey that requires patience, dedication, and love. It's not just about pampering your body, but also nourishing your mind and soul. When you fall in love with this process, you open yourself up to endless possibilities, and you are able to bring your best self to everything you do.

14

# be happy on your own

Taking time to be alone with your thoughts allows for a deeper journey of self-discovery. Solitude provides the space to reflect on your experiences, understand your emotions, and connect with your true self.

15

# eliminate negative self-talk

Start by listening to the voice inside your head. What is she saying? Take notes. Reflect and challenge. Catch your self-talk and replace it with a positive affirmation. Speak to yourself with generosity, forgiveness, positivity and love.

16

# check in with yourself

Self-reflection is a powerful tool that allows you to delve deeper into your inner self and discover hidden truths and insights. By understanding your thoughts, feelings, and behaviours, you unlock the power to make positive changes.

17

# create a bucket list

A bucket list reminds you that life is short and to make the most of it you need to be proactive. Brainstorm without limits. Write down everything that comes to mind. Set a timeframe and prioritise your three, five and ten items. Share the list with someone and designate activities you'd like to do together.

18

# give yourself a break

Next time you are giving yourself a hard time, give yourself a pat on your back. This simple act provides an easy way to forgive yourself and move on. It liberates the mind from dwelling on 'the problem' and frees up mental space for better use.

19

# take baby steps

Progress is often made by taking small, consistent actions towards your dreams. Like a jigsaw puzzle, each small piece may seem insignificant on its own, but when put together, it creates a beautiful and complete picture. Trust that every small step you take will lead you to great things.

> Great things are done by a series of small things done together.

VINCENT VAN GOGH

20

# put your oxygen mask on first

If you are a parent, you may find that idea challenging, because it goes against the grain to help yourself before helping your kids. But if you can't breathe you can't save others. Same for self-care, care for yourself before caring for others.

21

# be on your side

Each act of self-care strengthens the truest parts of who you are, while quieting the voice of doubt and fear. Create a space to reconnect with your authentic self and show up in the world with greater confidence.

22

# rethink your goals

Take a moment to assess your goals, are your goals realistic and relevant? Choose goals that support your growth and wellbeing, letting go of those that no longer align with your values. Don't stress about giving up on goals. Giving up on unrealistic and irrelevant goals will create space for you to really care about the other achievable ones.

23

# set boundaries

Boundaries are essential to safeguard your wellbeing, honour your values, and stay aligned with what truly matters to you. Protect your time and energy by setting healthy boundaries, and nurture relationships built on mutual respect and understanding.

24

# learn to say 'no'

As you try to meet the needs of others, saying 'no' is hard. Learn to say 'no' with confidence and certainty, it's a habit you need to cultivate. When saying no, say no. If you are feeling overloaded and on the edge, say that. Each "no" to what drains you is a "yes" to your peace.

25

# say 'goodbye' to toxic relationships

You deserve friendship and love from other people. If you are currently holding on to relationships that don't serve you, let them go. Don't let anyone rent a space in your head unless they're a good tenant. Unfollow, unfriend, delete, ignore.

26

# do more of what works for you

Design your own self-care plan. Ensure that you are making time for the things that matter, whether that's the boring stuff like setting your weekly meal plan, or the things you enjoy like pursuing a hobby. Do more of the things that get in touch with your authentic self.

27

# be the light

It's a beautiful thing to be able to do what you love. Whether it's a hobby or a profession, when you're engaged in something that brings you joy, it radiates from you. And that energy can inspire and awaken the hearts of those around you.

28

# enjoy life

Happiness often comes from the simple things you hold close. Take a moment to think of what pleases you, whether it's certain people, places or activities. Do more of them and less of the things that don't make you happy.

29

# indulge yourself

Everybody deserves a treat, perhaps it's a luxury spa treatment or beauty therapy, or perhaps you'd prefer to go for a walk on the beach or out for a delicious meal. Whatever you like to do, do it from time to time for no other reason than you want to.

30

# make time for each other

It's easy to forget about the one you love the most. Plan a special moment together, whether it's a big surprise or a simple date night, to honour the love you share. A good relationship with a partner is second only to a good relationship with yourself. Don't neglect it.

31

# get out in the nature

Walking in nature improves your mood and captivates your senses. It allows you to witness the beauty of the seasonal changes, the colours, the sounds, and the fresh air. It reminds you that you are all connected and part of something greater than yourself.

32

# learn something new

It's amazing how learning something new can spark creativity, often in ways you hadn't anticipated. Learning stimulates creativity as new information and new perspectives help you join the dots in new ways. Whether it's sport, musical instrument, craft activity or something heady like writing or blogging, learning a new skill is good for you.

33

# be dicsiplined

Self-care is about committing to do what needs to be done in order to stay healthy and balanced. Perhaps it's tuning the TV off at night, making a family budget, ending a toxic relationship or building a new career.

34

# wake up early

The hours before dawn hold a quiet magic, there's a stillness in the world that allows for fresh energy. Waking early can be a powerful way to harness this energy, allowing you to take a step ahead and feel connected to the world as it comes alive.

35

# meditate in the morning

Meditate when your mind is clear and free from the stresses of the day. Practice for however long as you like, but five minutes is a good start. It will help to set you up for the day, generating an overall sense of calm, and enable you to tackle the day with greater focus and energy.

36

# take a moment for your mantra

Say your chosen mantra to set the tone for the day and align yourself with your deepest desire. Bond with your mantra and make it your own. Chant it, speak it out loud in front of the mirror or write it down. It's a moment of connection with your true self as the day unfolds.

37

# savour your coffee

Observe the smell and the noise as your coffee brews. Fill the mug and pick it up, noting its warmth. Take a sip. Savour its smell and rich, earthy flavour. Notice the sensation in your mouth. Slowly but surely begin to tune into your day.

38

# drink plenty of water

Your body is always showing up for you, doing its magic to support you so you can enjoy life to the fullest. It needs water to survive. Now it's your turn to take care of your body. Count on eight cups a day, and drink.

39

# eat well

Like drinking water, nutrition is a foundation stone of survival. And like sleep, eating well is a simple but radical act of self-care. Eat the rainbow, eat all the colours of fruit and vegetables. Nourish your body by giving it what it needs to thrive.

40

# stretch

Stretching is a gift you give to your body and mind each morning. It keeps your muscles flexible, strong and healthy. It helps your blood flow and calms the mind. Set yourself a simple five-minute routine to do while the sun rises. You can even do it before you get out of bed.

41

# honour your body

Your body carries you through every experience, so don't forget to honour your body for its constancy. Your body is the home to your soul and your senses. It sustains you and brings you pleasure. Treat your body with the care and love it deserves.

42

# don't rush

Planning may seem time-consuming, but it can make you more productive in the long run. By taking the time to prioritise your tasks, you can work more efficiently, achieving your goals with greater ease.

*Rushing never saved the time that planning did.*

BEN PARRIS

43

# create a night-time ritual

Go to bed early and around the same time each night. Switch your phone one hour before bedtime, read a chapter of a book, take a relaxing bath, drink calming chamomile tea, and create a night-time ritual that help you ease into quality sleep.

*It is a common experience that a problem difficult at night is resolved in the morning after the committee of sleep has worked on it.*

JOHN STEINBECK

44

# find your motivation

Find work that matters to you because you do it for a reason that matters to you. That reason might be financial security, creative fulfilment, helping others or flexing a moral muscle. Understanding why you are doing something makes it easier to keep doing it, even on bad days.

45

# keep learning to grow your career

Continuous learning keeps your mind active, helps you adapt to new challenges, and brings fresh energy to your work. Read journals, join online networking groups, and take professional development courses. No matter what your position is, you can keep learning and growing.

46

# invest in yourself

Investing in yourself is one of the most meaningful commitments you can make. Read, watch, or do something that will help you grow. You're worth the time, money and effort. Time spent on nurturing yourself is never time wasted.

47

# set yourself up to work from home

Get a nice desk and a comfortable chair. Put up quotes, artwork or a vision board that inspires you or reminds you of the people and things that matter. Check emails at set times daily. Shut down your laptop at the end of your working day, change to your casual clothes and go for a walk.

48

# dress up just for yourself

You don't need a reason. If you feel that way, do it. Sometimes it makes you feel simply invincible to do your hair and make up, put on your favourite or most glamorous clothes and look the world right in the eye. Reconnect with your own power and present your best self to the world.

49

# go somewhere new

The world is your oyster. Traveling broadens your understanding of the world. When you see new places, interact with different people, and experience life outside of your routine, you open yourself to a deeper compassion and curiosity about other people.

50

# eliminate decisions

You make about 35,000 remotely conscious decisions a day. That's an incredible load on the brain. Free up some space by creating easy habits you can do automatically, such as locking in your exercise routine and planning meals ahead.

51

# sing at the top of your lungs

There's something magical about singing, whether it's in the shower, while driving, or in the company of friends. It lifts the spirit, frees the mind, and fills the air with joy. It's not just the melody, but the expression, the release, and the moment of harmony. Every note is a small celebration of life.

*52*

# create a positive playlist

Music is not confined to the limits of language or reason; it speaks directly to the soul. Its pure, raw energy can transform moods, heal wounds, and bring people together. Whether it's a simple melody or a complex symphony, music has a way of making you feel seen, heard, and understood.

*Music is probably the only real magic I have encountered in my life. There's not some trick involved with it. It's pure and it's real. It moves. It heals. It communicates and does all these incredible things.*

TOM PETTY

53

# create a vision board

Work out what inspires you and find a way to keep your inspiration top of mind. Collect quotes that resonate with you or photos that bring back a memory. Create a vision board, write or draw up your dream life, and place it on the wall of your home office.

54

# keep a journal

Journaling is a great way to untangle the worries that occupy your mind. When the page feels daunting, a simple prompt can be all it takes to get the pen moving. Journaling doesn't need to be perfect, sometimes, the act of writing itself opens doors to insights you never knew you had.

55

# start a mood tracker

A mood tracker can help you pause and think about what's going on. See your emotions represented visually and see how far you've come over time. It can help you pinpoint your feelings and make improvements to your daily life.

56

# make a cup of tea

Tea has a magical way of balancing the soul. It's a gentle companion to your emotions. Whether you seek warmth, coolness, calm, or cheer, tea has a remarkable ability to meet you exactly where you are. With every sip of tea, you find balance and peace.

57

# have a think

Find a new podcast to listen to, read an interesting article that makes you think and provides you with a fresh, different perspective. Pick up a book, whenever you read something that resonates, write the insight down so you don't forget.

58

# give to others

While earning a living is essential, it's the deeper connection to purpose that gives life its true meaning. When you focus on the value you provide to others, whether through kindness, support or creating something that enriches lives, you realise that fulfilment comes from how you contribute.

59

# send a love note

Whether it's a handwritten note or a thoughtful text, taking a moment to tell someone you love them is a small act that can leave a lasting impact. Life may be short, but love, when expressed, extends far beyond time.

60

# own your story

Your stories are unique and personal, shaped by your experiences, values, and beliefs. Owning your story means accepting and embracing all parts of yourself, including the flaws and mistakes. It takes courage to share your story, but it is through this act that you connect and inspire others.

61

# love yourself

Loving yourself is a process that requires patience, kindness and perseverance. Just as learning to walk, it involves taking small steps, falling, getting up again, and repeating until it becomes second nature.

Learning to love yourself is like learning to walk — essential, life-changing, and the only way to stand tall.

Vironika Tugaleva

62

# call an old friend

It's easy to assume that reaching out feels like an imposition, but in reality, reconnecting is often a simple joy for both sides. A phone call without any agenda, just to say hello, is a reminder that relationships are built on moments of genuine connection, not on expectations.

63

# hygge your home

Hygge's travelled a long way from its native Danmark to teach people all around the globe how to get cozy in their special way. Invest in furniture and lights that you love. Create a reading nook. Put up a nice photo or artwork. Declutter. Destress. And enjoy.

64

# take care of small tasks

It's amazing how quickly small tasks can pile up and weigh on your mind. Take a moment to handle them when they arise. If a task takes less than two minutes to complete, take care of it right away. Designate a block of time in your weekly calendar to tackle more complicated tasks.

65

# relax without an agenda

Set aside blocks of time in your diary solely for you. Use the slot to do nothing at all. This is not the time to clean or cook or catch up on unread emails. It's the time to add to your mood board or flick through a magazine. Enjoy personal time without an agenda.

66

# do nothing

It can be easy to forget to unplug from your daily routines. But just like any electronic device, you also need a break to recharge. Disconnecting from your screens, work, and other distractions can help you refresh your mind, relax your body, and gain a new perspective on your life.

*Almost everything will work again if you unplug it for a few minutes, including you.*

ANNE LAMOTT

67

# sleep well and laugh loudly

A good laugh can uplift your spirits, release tension, and bring joy to your life. Likewise, a restful sleep allows your body to recharge, repair, and find balance. In the face of life's challenges, you can find solace and restoration in the healing powers of laughter and quality sleep.

68

# eat sustainably

Try to buy your local farmers' produce, be aware of food miles and connect with the land around you. Try to eat seasonally, find out what's growing now and tailor your meal plan accordingly. Honouring the earth's natural rhythms and reducing your environmental footprint.

69

# go out and take photos

Photography offers you a unique way to pause and truly observe what's around you. Choose your subject carefully and look at it before you press the shutter. Taking a photo attunes you to your environment, improves memory and helps you to focus on meaningful experiences.

70

# let it go

Life is full of ups and downs, and sometimes you may find yourself carrying burdens that are not yours to bear. You have a choice in what you carry. Let go of the things that weigh you down and make space for the things that bring you joy and peace.

71

# don't focus on being nice

Your inner peace is more important than social obligation. Protect it unapologetically. It's not your job to smile at strangers, join in conversations, like posts on social media or agree to participate in things you don't want to do. Remember that.

72

# compliment yourself

Put pen to paper and list all the things that you love about yourself. Make a note of your skills and specialties to remind yourself that you are talented, wonderful and worthy. Remember to add more to the list as you grow and refer to it when you're feeling low.

*73*

# reclaim your inner peace

Your inner peace should be treasured and protected. It can be easy to overlook the subtle ways your peace is chipped away. Learn to release what no longer aligns with your peace, and let go of the relationships, commitments, or routines that do not serve you any more.

74

# be your own best friend forever

Treat yourself the way you would treat your best friend. Shower yourself with praise and encouragement. It is not selfish or unkind to prioritise yourself and your needs. You can't pour from an empty cup, so make sure yours is full of something delicious.

75

# you are worthy of compassion

It is easy to prioritise the needs of others, but true compassion encompasses your own wellbeing as well. When you show yourself kindness, understanding, and forgiveness, you cultivate a deeper sense of self-love, allowing you to extend genuine compassion to others.

76

# be kinder to yourself

When you treat yourself with kindness, you replenish your spirits and create a reservoir of love and compassion that can overflow into the world around you. So when you fail and fall, someone will be by your side, wipe up your tears and fears away, and help you stand stronger.

77

# pause and thank yourself

Pause every now and then to thank yourself. Thank your body for keeping you alive every day. Thank your mind for being creative and logical. Thank your sense of humour for keeping you sane. Show yourself love and gratitude for just being you.

78

# forgive yourself

Each mistake is an opportunity to learn and grow. Instead of dwelling on past errors, step back to see what the situation can teach you. Once you have acknowledged the mistake and chosen to learn from it, move on.

79

# celebrate the chaos

Life is a messy tapestry of imperfections. It's in the chaos that you find the most profound moments of growth and self-discovery. Embrace the glorious mess that you are, with all your flaws, quirks, and vulnerabilities. Recognising that your imperfections are what make you authentic.

80

# be helped

Asking for help is often harder than it seems. By requesting assistance, you acknowledge the immense benefits of support. Good friends will be more than happy to lend a hand if you ask. Be open to receiving it.

81

# get what you give

Love is a reflection of your capacity to give and receive, and it starts with you. Love is not solely about receiving; it's about giving selflessly and unconditionally, without expecting anything in return. When you choose to love, you invite love into your life and inspire others to do the same.

82

# respect your values

You hold your opinions for a reason. Keep promises to yourself and trust in your own values. It is important not to let your opinions be dictated or belittled by others. An open mind and a strong will are destined to take you far.

83

# fall in love with yourself

Loving yourself is a lifelong romance with yourself, where you prioritise your wellbeing, set healthy boundaries, and nourish your mind and body. Loving yourself allows you to show up authentically in the world, attract healthy relationships, and navigate life's challenges with greater resilience.

*To love oneself is the beginning of a life-long romance.*

OSCAR WILDE

84

# take the wheel

It can be difficult to know which path is right for you, but the important thing is that you take ownership of your choices. While it can be scary, it's also incredibly empowering. Embrace your autonomy and start charting your own course. The possibilities are endless.

85

# let yourself feel

Take some time to process and come to terms with how you feel. Acknowledge your emotions and work out why you feel a certain way. Don't push upset and frustration down, let them surface. It helps you get to the root cause of the problem and deal with it thoroughly.

86

# feed the soul

When you take the time to enjoy a delicious meal, you engage your senses, savouring the flavours, textures, and aromas that bring you joy. A satisfying meal can uplift your mood, spark conversations, and create cherished memories.

87

# look out for the vulnerable

Friendship is more than shared laughter and good times; it's about being a pillar of strength when someone you care about is facing difficulties. Sometimes, all a friend needs is the reassurance that someone is truly there for them, offering a safe and judgment-free space.

*88*

# start with empathy

Every person you meet, no matter how different they may seem, carries their own burdens and battles. Kindness is a bridge that connects us, reminding us of our shared humanity and the common thread of struggle. Through acts of kindness, you can create a ripple effect of compassion and support.

89

# teach a man to fish

Every act of kindness, no matter how small, can make a difference in someone's life. Whether it's a warm smile, a listening ear, or a simple gesture of support, these small acts can touch hearts, inspire others, and contribute to a more compassionate and connected world.

90

# send snail mail

A letter holds more than words, it carries thought, care, and a piece of the sender's spirit. Pen your pal a little letter telling them you miss them or reminiscing about a fun memory. It's the little acts of kindness that make someone's day.

91

# be encouraged

Life is a journey filled with dreams, and often it is the support of the right people that helps you turn them into reality. Surround yourself with individuals who believe in you, uplift you, and stand by your side. They provide the encouragement, guidance, and strength you need to reach for the stars.

92

# forgive someone

The best way to let go of resentment is to replace it with kindness and love. You have the power to end the storm and bring about calm. Hanging on to pain and grudges only contributes to anger. Make peace with your present moment and let go of the past.

93

# thank someone

Thank people for everything they do for you, from passing you the salt shaker to fixing your laptop. Giving thanks is the best habit to develop. Not only does it make the person who helped you feel good, but it also makes them more willing to help you again.

94

# spread the love

Your words and actions may fade from memory over time, but the way you make others feel has a lasting impact. The true essence of your interactions lies in the emotions you evoke within others. You have the power to touch hearts, inspire change, and create meaningful connections that endure beyond the moment.

*People will forget what you said. People will forget what you did, but people will never forget how you made them feel.*

MAYA ANGELOU

95

# hug it out

Hugs, those gentle embraces that connect people, hold a remarkable power to nourish your wellbeing. They go beyond simple physical contact and become a language of love, comfort, and support. They can sustain you, maintain your balance, and even foster your growth.

96

# consider your words

The way you describe your life can change the way you feel about it. Words like blessing, blessed, gift, lucky, fortunate, abundance, appreciate, value, treasure... Be aware of how you use words when talking about your life, and try introducing some of these thankful words into your vocabulary.

97

# stay beautiful

To have beautiful eyes, seek and appreciate the goodness in those around you. Beautiful lips are adorned with words of kindness, uplifting and inspiring others. And to embody poise, you carry yourself with the assurance that you are supported, never alone in this journey called life.

98

# be always kind

You are inherently worthy of compassion and kindness, simply by virtue of being human. Your existence, with all its complexities, triumphs, and struggles, is enough. There's no need to prove your worthiness to earn love.

99

# be gentle

While force may impose temporary changes, it is through kindness that lasting transformations occur. When you approach others with compassion, understanding, and generosity, you create a connection that brings about positive change.

100

# pursue your best life

You only have one life, so make sure you prioritise chasing your dreams and honouring your desires. The challenges will teach you, the achievements will complete you, and the memories will be treasured forever.

101

# make your day

Today is a new day, a fresh start, a chance to rewrite your story. It's a day to eat well, to exercise, and to nurture your mind and soul. It's a day to choose health, happiness, and purpose. It's a day to be intentional, to live with passion and pride, and to pursue your dreams relentlessly.

Today is your day.
To start fresh.
To eat right.
To train hard.
To live healthy.
To be proud.

BONNIE PFIESTER

# from Cecilia

Through daily rituals, words of empowerment, and affirming quotes, I hope to support and inspire you to live your dream life filled with moments of reflection, self-discovery, and love.

If you found this book helpful, please review and share it. That helps it find its way to those who need it. This would mean a lot to me. Thank you.

Connect with me:
https://thedreamlifeproject.co
◉ @dreamlifeproject_

www.ingramcontent.com/pod-product-compliance
Lightning Source LLC
Chambersburg PA
CBHW061750070526
44585CB00025B/2848